RHYME CRAFT

Essex Poets

Edited By Daisy Job

First published in Great Britain in 2018 by:

YoungWriters

Young Writers
Remus House
Coltsfoot Drive
Peterborough
PE2 9BF
Telephone: 01733 890066
Website: www.youngwriters.co.uk

FOREWORD

Welcome Reader, to *Rhymecraft - Essex Poets*.

Among these pages you will find a whole host of poetic gems, built from the ground up by some wonderful young minds. Included are a variety of poetic styles, from amazing acrostics to creative cinquains, from dazzling diamantes to fascinating free verse.

Here at Young Writers our objective has always been to help children discover the joys of poetry and creative writing. Few things are more encouraging for the aspiring writer than seeing their own work in print. We are proud that our anthologies are able to give young authors this unique sense of confidence and pride in their abilities as well as letting their poetry reach new audiences.

The editing process was a tough but rewarding one that allowed us to gain an insight into the blooming creativity of today's primary school pupils. I hope you find as much enjoyment and inspiration in the following poetry as I have, so much so that you pick up a pen and get writing!

Daisy Job

CONTENTS

Lewis Daniel London (10)	70
Ciarán JS Hinds (9)	71
Grace Wilkinson (10)	72
Phoebe Jones (10)	73
Sanjit Veeramreddy (10)	74
Reuben Jack Taylor (7)	75
Jacob Reed (10)	76
Charlotte Holmes (11)	77
Grace Alden (10)	78
Emily Windsor (10)	79
Abi Barratt (10)	80
Amelia Chatten (10)	81
Owen Ross (10)	82
Phoebe Ella Coles (7)	83
Thomas William Harvey (9)	84
Lilly-Mai Webster (7)	85
Riley Michael Abrehart (7)	86

Riverside Primary School, Hullbridge

Georgia Sydney Elizabeth Richards (11)	87
Ruby May Bence (9)	88
Ronnie Durussel (9)	90
Jessica Doyle (10)	91
Roman Foster (8)	92
Emma Potter (10)	93
Hollie Durussel (7)	94
Alfie McDonnell (10)	95
Hannah Grace Mealing (8)	96
Tyne Every (9)	97
Morgan Hunt (9)	98
Kaysie Colston (11)	99
Micky Woods (11)	100
Zach Land (10)	101
Ralph Hall (7)	102
Kayla Harris (9)	103
Lilia Gilbert (10)	104
Daisy Land (7)	105

Willowbrook Primary School, Hutton

Jack Oscar Harding (9), Samuel Reece Woodcock, Lucia Russell, Taylor & Alfie Pyner	106
Alexia Kendall (10)	108
Aryan Hussain (9)	110
Kai Jassy-Catton (9)	112
George Holloway (9)	114
Amelia Pixie Harding (9)	116
Dylan Hutchins (9)	118
Tim Baygeldi (8)	120
Sunni Bhundia (9)	121
Megan Lee (9)	122
Oscar Amos (9)	124
Cody Parish (9)	125
Jodie McGill (7)	126
Maisie Cocklin (11)	127
Hannah Baygeldi (7)	128
Skyla Lynch (10)	129
Faiqa Latheef (8)	130
Theo Pease (8)	131
Scarlett Wilkes (10)	132
Jessica Foster (11)	133
Lily-Maye Attree (8)	134
Leila Lynch (9)	135
Daisy Marshall (10)	136
Izzy Proctor (8)	137
Olivia Kamin (7)	138
Rachael Kilvington (10)	139
Ethan Metcalfe (10)	140
Ronnie Dowrich (10)	141
Rogue Marie Knight (8)	142
Mia Reisman (7)	143
Summer Sky Wild (10)	144
Matthew Magarinos (11)	145
Charlie Barber (7)	146
Benjamin Latchford (10)	147
Georgina Chappell (8)	148
Katie Harris (10)	149
Jack Brown (8)	150
Jamie Willis (9)	151
Tahlia Anne Cook (9)	152

Rubyrose Carmen-Jane Barlow (7)	153
Tommy Chitty (8)	154
Frankie Jobson (11)	155
Ellie Cross (8)	156
Theo Tsingano (8)	157
William Andrew Johnson (10)	158
Teddy Fleming (10)	159
Sophie Elizabeth White (11)	160
Risviny Thirunavugarasu (10)	161
Daniel Grundon (7)	162
Tom Proctor (7)	163
Farheen Saleel (10)	164
Amy Tobin (7)	165
Athina Kapralou (7)	166
Jack Moore (7)	167
Markella Ntisiou (7)	168
Nithilany Thirunavugarasu (7)	169
Isabelle Vosper (7)	170

Woodford Green Primary School, Woodford Green

Osman Nuri Aydin (9)	171
Ali Hasnan Mahmood (9)	172
Luke Marshall (9)	174

THE POEMS

Summer Is Horrible

Merrily, the sun comes out early in the morning,
It's joyful arms spread around the sky.
She smiles, skips and hops,
And sings a song until they wake up.
The sea's waves clash together,
Until the sand was wet and soggy.

Suddenly, the weather changes, the sun gets hotter.
Each second searching everything in its eyesight.
Her body is burning on the beach,
As well as the sun beds.
She is never cold-hearted
Always warm and burning.
Its teeth changing the colour of our shoes,
She's smirking away to the ground.
Her laser eyes burning our backs.
Its wilderness was over the top.
Her rusty lava fingers burning our legs till they are burnt.

Tanyaradzwa Gutsire (11)
Montgomery Junior School, Colchester

Rose Garden

Spring
The rose garden is rapidly blooming
Wearing a beautiful dress bright and light.
The rose garden was happily smiling,
knowing there won't be winter to have a fight.

Summer
The rose garden is very elegant now
Hugging all the trees enthusiastically
She was giving a curtsey and a bow
Prancing and dancing with plenty of ecstasy.

Autumn
She knows she's slowly, fading away,
But she won't give up; not today.
She will rise up with all her power.
To not let winter take her over.

Winter
She thought she could, no she couldn't
She fell to a cold grave.

She seriously shouldn't.
But it's too late now, next time she'll behave.

Spring
The rose garden is rapidly blooming
Wearing a beautiful dress bright and light
The rose garden was happily smiling.
knowing there won't be winter to fight.

Rochelle Benyin (10)
Montgomery Junior School, Colchester

Giant Winter

It's that time of year again.
The frost giant winter has awoken from his
slumber.
He forces animals into a deep sleep.

He shakes the trees with his icy breath.
He creeps into the cold chilly air, he brings to the
world.
Giant Winter watches the trees
And plants die with a twisted expression.
The monstrosity decorates the trees with white
velvet.
And icicles which are the trees frozen tears.

The infamous creature whispers to children,
Making them dirty deeds,
Icicles for fingers, black eyes
And at his back was Death.

Although his frost thaws
His icicles lost grip on the world
The giant of life, spring, was taking over,
Oh how Winter despised Spring.

He wouldn't comprehend Spring.
He crawled back to his den to slumber for another year.

Ashley Kandawasvika (10)
Montgomery Junior School, Colchester

Autumn Leaves

Autumn's leaving home today,
Sadly sobbing, dreading her long adventure to the
under earth.
Leaves bouncing on the branches,
Whilst holding onto their forever home,
living on a tree.
Leave was anxiously waiting for her wave off
To the under earth.

Autumns leaves time has nearly come
She's feeling sad and nervous,
To say her goodbye to her family and friends.
The pile of autumn leaves are getting bigger
and bigger.
The pile awaits her,
Leaves go on her adventure.

She sadly and slowly,
Drops, into the pile of leaves,
Feeling depressed, angry and sad.
She finally drops into the colourful pile of leaves.
She is now in the middle of the beautiful autumn
leaves.

So, then this is how the life of colourful autumn leaves work.

Lola Stoneley (11)
Montgomery Junior School, Colchester

Tsunami

The tsunami rises from the sea like an elevator
He charges to crush anything in its path.
He smothers other buildings to make them bow
He drowns stuff with a mega wave.
Devastating lives at a mega cost
He charges with a monstrous look.
Conquering land with his watery hands
Carelessly floods towns and cities
Moves plants, decorations and objects.
He eats everything up like a tornado.
Racing to destroy buildings in his path
Viciously he screams with his watery throat
Selfishly he wiped out the city for no reason
Then the tsunami calmed down and went away.

Aiden Henning (10)
Montgomery Junior School, Colchester

Life As A Tree

Swiftly, the tree moves her arms with the wind,
As the sap spills out of her weeping,
She grows and grows as the sun moves across the sky.
Yet she still feels trapped in her rooty shoes,
She stretches out to give the world a hug,
As she stretches her bark splits,
While she stands silently watching the world.
She feels like her leaves are jewellery,
As the tree dances with the wind,
She solemnly sits there waiting and waiting.
But as winter got closer her leaves were collapsing onto the floor,
As she anxiously waited for winter to go,
Her bark fell off day by day.

Alara Janet Wilson (10)
Montgomery Junior School, Colchester

Lightning

Lightning was everyone's idol
Racing, waving to the crowds
Joyously streaking through the mystical, magical sky.
Everyone was jealous and admired him.
Chasing the clouds enthusiastically.
He cheerfully and happily jumps out of the soft clouds and screeches wildly.
Poking out and showing his new neon shiny yellow coat.
A flash below the clouds.
Touching them very gently.

The storm is finally over, it's all silent
While the destruction is noticed.
Everything is broken, trees, cars and even homes.
Nothing escaped...

Kian Lewis (11)
Montgomery Junior School, Colchester

Autumn

Astonishing autumn getting prepared for the new
day to begin,
Delaying for something to say.
Becoming undressed from her delightful leaves,
shaking her dress off.
Gradually, smoothing the world with wonderful
dress
So wonderful that such a thing has been created
by her.

Introducing, her gush of breath
Giggling, as the special squirrel dances up on her
arm.
Behaving weakly, shyly
And carefully as she dresses the world
Shaking, dancing, skipping.
Chanting, chanting, chanting to winter to get
ready and show his fall.

Ashlee Rose Ninnim (11)
Montgomery Junior School, Colchester

Hurricane

The thunderous hurricane had woken from her glorious slumber.
Ready to cause trouble.
The queen of destruction, she called herself,
Ready to cause disaster, racing, zooming, dashing,
Devouring anything in her path as she laughed and giggled,
Frantically spinning and dancing.
Hungrily destroying everything while turning and cheering.
She looked behind her shoulder, realised what she had done.
Her face turned solemn and collapsed onto the ground
Ready to emerge again.

Elsie Adjei-Adebi (10)
Montgomery Junior School, Colchester

The Big Storm

Yearly, storm comes,
This year storm is waiting to come out
And so he came out
He pushed, pulled anything in its way.
Destroying homes as he moved forward.
Whooshing birds back to front,
You could hear citizens screaming for their lives,
While they're hearing the clash
And clangs of thunder and lightning.

It is known that storms drop out of sight in days,
So, it keeps going, *clash*, clangs of thunder
And lightning.

Hakeem Daho (10)
Montgomery Junior School, Colchester

Earthquake

Earthquake has left home,
Sad, angry and aggressive,
He comes dashing, zooming and stomping,
Destroying the whole land,
Pieces are left crumbled and scrambled,
Oh, how would the world be now?
Shaking and making noises, however scary could
get it now.

Destructive he comes,
Looking for some food, waiting for people to come.
Boom! Clash! Rumble! Mumble!
You know that there is trouble.
Here he comes, watch out.

Sharon Shosanya (10)
Montgomery Junior School, Colchester

Lightning Storm

Lightning storm has woken up from his sleep.
Dashes as he rushes to the city.
He trembles as he strikes lots of people
And animals out of the way.
Carelessly he kills lots of people.
Lightning storm is growing bigger with his pride,
He's happy that he's 'king of the storm,'
He grins as he kills lots of people.
Rapidly, lightning storm knocks down mountains,
Buildings and planets.
He smirks as he breaks lots of homes.

Joe Oakley (11)
Montgomery Junior School, Colchester

Garden

Garden is losing her flowers today,
She cried herself to sleep last night,
Cried, cried, cried in the moonlight.

She constantly loses her grassy coat,
Courageously, she devoured her soil slowly,
Slowly, slowly, slowly in the daylight,
As she sheds her tears.

She waves goodbye to her friends the daisy twins,
Everyone has left the small city,
City, city, city and through the gate.

Megan-Rose Walford (11)
Montgomery Junior School, Colchester

Hurricane

Hurricane is the destroyer of people,
Nothing can resist its hunger,
If you get in its way you get the thunder,
If you stay, It can be lethal.

Hurricane is loud,
Hurricane is strong,
Hurricane is dangerous
And is not fun.

Hurricane dashes past the trees,
He rudely rushes through all the buildings,
Then he dies due to exhaustion.

Liam Duffy (10)
Montgomery Junior School, Colchester

Snowfall

Rapidly racing down the hundred foot fall,
He's in front deciding to hit the ground first,
In his head, he is thinking,
I cannot wait to make those children so happy.
Eventually he hits the ground,
Anxiously he waits,
The children hurry to model him into something,
He loves being modelled then destroyed again into
a humongous mess.

Frazer Wallace (10)

Montgomery Junior School, Colchester

Lava

Rapidly charging towards the city destroying
buildings,
And chasing your dreams away,
Turning them into nightmares.

It's not a pretty sight to see people racing away,
From the terror screaming out for help.

Racing upon the motorway, eating away at cars,
Leaving his anger behind.

Toby Land
Montgomery Junior School, Colchester

Storms Are Boss

Storm has been awoken, the one that strongly
Strangles the houses,
Madly, the city-eating storm went from city to city,
Crossly, foolishly killing the joyful lives.
Angrily chucking things in his way,
Tossing homes with the wind's breath,
Madly crying with his rain,
Storm has been destroyed.

Alfie Gutteridge (10)
Montgomery Junior School, Colchester

Thunder And Lightning

Thunder and lightning, loud and scary
Dashing down from the sky like a madman
Screaming, setting forests on fire
Then goes away for another day
Unfortunately they return to ruin the day
Everyone is sad and scared so they go to sleep
Every clash wakes people up.

Shane Casey (10)
Montgomery Junior School, Colchester

Storms

Rapidly banging on the door like a gunshot.
Ripping bits to pieces as it was the Hulk.
She danced from the sky like a ballerina.
Sobbing with tears.
Soaring from the sky like the blades of a helicopter.
Destroying everything like a wrecking ball.

Archie Ashcroft (10)

Montgomery Junior School, Colchester

Monkey Adventures

In the jungle there's a monkey lurking,
It swings and swings all around the trees.
The monkey is brown and cheeky.
It can easily escape from danger.
It's really fluffy and very cute.
It likes eating bananas
And its favourite food is a Mint Club.
Look at him go!
As he swings across the trees, he is so fast!
He swings and swings and swings, you can't catch him,
No, he's too fast!
He never gets tired, run, run as fast as you can
Or the lion will get you!
The monkey got away from that beastly animal.
The monkey is so proud that he got away.
The monkey rests by curling his tail around a branch.
His eyes that are small, slowly close
And he finally gets some sleep.
'What a day!' he said.

Elliot Reed (7)

Prettygate Junior School, Colchester

Gods In Pots

Do you see those gods in pots sir?
Do you think they're gods from Greece, sir?
No, I think they're gods in pots, sir.
Do you know their great names, sir?
Well their names are Hades, the god of death, not
a very nice guy.
I think his real name could be Beth or Death
himself;
Let's move on to Poseidon, now he's big like a
mother pig and he digs his waves and earthquakes
like no mother pig.
So let's dig onto the next one, Zeus the dad of the
gods.
Not a bad one, no he's the god of storms and stuff,
I don't like him that much.
So let's sing some more rhymes, no, OK.
Next Athena, god of wisdom, to be god of
wisdom's very good.
So, let's recap a god of death not Macbeth.
A mountain waves, a gigantic thunder of yellow
and white, oh boy, what a fright.

A bunch of wisdom and a bit of boiling ruby-red
fire, if we add Apollo god of the sun.
And that's the end of our tour of gods in pots sir.

Nathan Smith (9)

Prettygate Junior School, Colchester

Skeletons

In a Minecraft World there was a person
called Steve,
And he saw some trees, so he started
punching them.
But in a cave a skeleton was watching him.
Steve made a table that was made for crafting.
But then the skeleton shot him and Steve died.
The world was on hard-core mode,
so he had to start a new world.
Steve was annoyed, but he went to punch
some trees.
It was getting dark soon so Steve decided to stay
in a cave for the night.
He placed down a crafting table
and furnace and a bed,
He went to sleep.
But, then a skeleton appeared
and shot Steve and he died.
Then he re-spawned in a new world.

But as soon as Steve spawned a creeper
blew him up and he died.
Then he quit.

Logan Green (9)
Prettygate Junior School, Colchester

My Day At The Farm

At the farm there were lots of sheep.
And one of the sheep went *baaa*,
And I got scared and I went weep!
It was cold because it was winter but soon it will
be summer.
There were lots of pigs rolling in the mud.
I thought they were swimming in a flood.
There were some cats and dogs.
The dogs barked and the cats purred at me.
I milked the cows
And I made milk for people to drink.
Ducks were swimming in a pond, going round and
round.
What a lovely day it has been, I thought to myself,
As I walked home for tea.

Joelle Frimpong (8)
Prettygate Junior School, Colchester

Daydreams

All I can imagine today,
The scent of the flowery trees,
The prettiness of the roses nearby,
And the happiness of the lovely breeze.

Sunrise to sunset,
All the day and all the night,
Daylight beaming onto my face
Until the light is in my sight.

I think of every precious hour,
As it vanishes just like a flower,
Then it starts to fade away!

All I imagined today,
I smelt the flowery trees
I took a glimpse of the pretty roses
And the happiness of the lovely breeze...

Iqra Zafar (10)
Prettygate Junior School, Colchester

The First Day In Your Life

In Camelot, where the snow fell something awoke.
So build your fort up high prepare forces for battle.
There is the enormous dragon on the loose!
With embers with their own song.
One spark could set your house on fire!
So build your house stern and strong.
Everyone has been defeated.
Hope yours will be lucky, but only a crazy fool
would ride on his own,
And of course, he was gone in a flash.
But after the winter was gone, the dragon was
gone too.
'Who killed the beast?'
I said, 'The knight.'

Zachary William Stevens (9)

Prettygate Junior School, Colchester

Bright Fireworks In The Night Sky

F antastic lights in the night sky

I lluminates everything around.

R emember to stay away when they're shooting off!

E njoy the wonderful colours bursting out in the sky.

W ondrous fireworks in all shapes and sizes,

O oh and ahh you will hear as they bang in the sky

R ising up into the night sky, trust me, you'll love it!

K nowing you're safe, just sit back and enjoy

S himmering and shining you won't want to miss it!

Isabel Lambert (9)

Prettygate Junior School, Colchester

ower Is To Find

Coltan
Is in iPhones
and also everywhere,
Coltans in technology
But not found in the air,
There are not just positive things
Animals becoming extinct
Children dying from falling rocks
There goes your phone... *Ring!*

Power
Is in Coltan
Crazy people mining it
Sold for millions of pounds each time
In Congo, find it!
Destroying poor animals habitats
Diseases spreading fast
Innocent kids dying now, Coltan has to last!

Poppy Ganderton (10)
Prettygate Junior School, Colchester

The Story Of A Gorilla

A gorilla.
As mad as the sun.
As loud as a radio that has been turned on.
As horrid as a bully.
As awesome as a gangster.
As fast as a cheetah.
He is as big as a building.
More grumpy than a Viking.
His teeth are as sharp as knives.
He's got a fluffy coat.
His mouth is as big as a rhino's head.
More selfish than a crab.
It's chest is as strong as a brick.
As vicious as a piranha.
His head is bigger than a brick.

Dexter Chisnall (8)
Prettygate Junior School, Colchester

Unicorn

A big fluffy coat and a sharpened horn
on top of its cute little head.
It trots like a horse, but a tiny bit faster.
It shines like shiny glitter on a piece of paper.
Are you not surprised? What an amazing sight!
It eats chocolate and sweets, mmmm, delicious!
Galloping, sprinting and leaping into the forest
as happy as me,
And as bright as the sun.
Oh and how clean it is,
You probably don't have to wash it
for a whole three years.

Ruby Mae Hill (7)
Prettygate Junior School, Colchester

The Deep Sea

In the ocean I know where I must be,
For I must swim in the deep, dark sea.
It wants me to join it in the blue vast world,
On land I feel trapped like in a zoo.
And I know the sea will set me free.
I see the things of dreams as the waves lap.
I kick and hear the sea's song.
Swimming feels long as I slow down calmly.
I love it as the land is a pong.
The sea is perfume and it will be my wonder
forever to never let it go.

Freddie Leech (9)

Prettygate Junior School, Colchester

Dragons

Dragons fly, roaming the Earth,
Up in the sky, beneath the surf.
Breathing fire, or shooting ice;
Some are mean and some are nice.

Underground or up in trees,
Hiding there amongst the leaves.
Some are strong and some are weak;
Every one of them is unique.

Golden, silver, green or brown,
Flying up and diving down.
Covered in scales or leathery skin;
I'm sure that they make quite a din.

Jamie Derrick (10)
Prettygate Junior School, Colchester

The Minecraft Hobbies

I'm in the cave trying to get some diamonds,
I think I'm gonna hit some lava
But I don't care because Minecraft is the place to be.

I'm building a mansion that we all need,
I'm getting my blocks as quick as a flash,
I don't want creepers coming in a dash.

Attacking all the spiders climbing up the walls
Fighting zombies up and down,
Never gonna stop
Never gonna stop!

Daniel Thomas Potter (10)
Prettygate Junior School, Colchester

My Little Cousin

My little cousin
She's a real brat,
My little cousin
She pees on my mat.

My little cousin
She's almost in nursery,
My little cousin
She still has a potty.

My little cousin
She just learnt how to walk,
My little cousin
I wonder when she'll talk.

My little cousin
Although she is only three,
My little cousin
I know she still loves me.

Claudia Martin (8)
Prettygate Junior School, Colchester

Science

Hydrogen, helium, oxygen, magnesium
they are all from the table of elements.
Sun, Mercury, Venus, Earth, Mars,
they are all planets.
Solids, liquids and gasses,
everything is made of at least one of these.
Methane is a gas, it is also referred to as farts or
toots that smell like fruits.
A brick is a solid, a brick is thick.
Water is a liquid, it can also be referred to as H20...
Yo!

George Webber (9)
Prettygate Junior School, Colchester

Dogs

Dogs are amazing,
You get a glimpse of pink from a poodle,
A look of black from a sausage dog
And a little light brown from a pug.
Cocker spaniels and springers,
All as fast as a cheetah.
Some dogs black, some white
That go to bed well in the night.
The German shepherd faster than the Dalmatian.
Also the sharp claws of all of the dogs.
They really are amazing dogs!

Sophie Potter (7)
Prettygate Junior School, Colchester

Untitled

M illions of very happy players

I nterestingly, you can play on iPhones, iPads, you can play on anything

N aughty some people can be

E xtremely fun game

C an craft coolness

R oaring pigs gobbling mountains of grass

A mazing game physics

F unny animals eating, exploding

T he Ender Dragon and Withers destroying everything.

Benjamin Latter (10)

Prettygate Junior School, Colchester

Leo The Lion

He has one hairy mane
Four little legs,
One very waggy tail
And teeth as sharp as blades
His roar is oh so loud,
That you can hear it from miles away
He is a very big meat eater.
He is king of the jungle and all around
He is also the king of nearly every animal in the world
He is a very scary animal,
Maybe the scariest in the whole jungle.

Maya Pearl Coulter (7)
Prettygate Junior School, Colchester

My Hobby

H ey listen up, listen to my hobby

O h yeah! about my dance teacher

B e careful that you don't twist your ankle

B ut if you don't you'll be thankful

I rather like street and slow dancing, but I like to

E ngage in art as well but sometimes I don't have a clue what to draw

S o I drew me drawing a drawer.

Sophie McNamara (10)
Prettygate Junior School, Colchester

Cheetah

Four legs running,
Getting tired as they go,
Two ears, cunning,
He won't stop, no!
Running, plodding, stepping,
Fluffy and stripy
Fast as a shooting star!

He's running past the trees,
Using his four legs,
Cheetah will run past you or I
Striding, leaping, limping,
Rough and spotty
Going fast as the wind!

Finley Lucas (7)
Prettygate Junior School, Colchester

Butterfly

Sparkly wings and shiny colours with sparkly legs.
It has twenty-one tiny legs and tiny teeth.
In their tiny, tiny mouth, there's a tiny smile.
They eat pollen.
Their friends are bees.
They make honey.
A butterfly is like a delicate angel.
A butterfly is like a graceful fairy.
A butterfly is as crazy as a fly.

Amelie Reed (7)
Prettygate Junior School, Colchester

Minecraft

Digging diamonds deep below,
Skeletons snipe and creepers explode,
I hold my pickaxe in my hand,
And shovel back to the air of the land,
Building my house of cobblestone,
But I have no friends, I live alone,
Zombies, spiders, Endermen,
Come and haunt my house again,
I'll kill them in the end.

Robert Southin (8)
Prettygate Junior School, Colchester

Football

F antastic football

O ffside rule is a strict rule

O ver the ref's decision he has the tool

T o give you a card

B e happy and enjoy the game

A lways obey the ref's decision

L ike you are listening to your teacher

L ove football like never before.

Junior Saunders Osei (9)

Prettygate Junior School, Colchester

I'm A Fabulous Monkey

A very skinny body,
Two little, tired arms,
Swinging, springing, leaping from one tree to
another.
The monkey is as bendy as a piece of rubber,
He smells of sweet roses and sugar.
The fabulous monkey is as fluffy as a cloud,
A monkey is like a burglar stealing bananas
that is a skinny mini monkey.

Georgia Motarski (7)
Prettygate Junior School, Colchester

The Firework Pop

Bang, pop, fizz you see me soaring into the night
My colours red, blue and green,
I'm sure you'll agree,
I'm the most beautiful firework you've ever seen,
Crash, bang! Boom!
You see me exploding in the sky,
Zooming right up high,
Everybody cheering as I fly.

Jessica Lemon (9)
Prettygate Junior School, Colchester

Awesome Animals

A nimals are amazing

N o animal is the same

I n the rain or in the sun, I love them anyway

M y life would be great, if I had a furry friend

A pet to be by my side every single day

L ovely and fluffy, kind and cute

S omething like... a little Jack Russell.

Erin Elsted (9)

Prettygate Junior School, Colchester

Orcas

Lots of sharp teeth to tackle large prey,
One blowhole to make more water,
One huge fin to swim fast,
Sneaky, cut-throat, dangerous,
Quiet, ferocious.
Teeth as sharp as knives,
Hunting in the night,
Its favourite meal is fresh seal,
Travels in a pack in the arctic ocean.

Jacob Knapp (7)
Prettygate Junior School, Colchester

The Night

T he night is relaxing
H appy dreams are everywhere
E ven the wind is sleeping

N othing can wake you
I will slumber till it is over
G ates are shut with bolts
H uge beasts snoozing
T ick-tock goes the clock.

Alexander Derrick (7)

Prettygate Junior School, Colchester

Wonderful Winter Poem

W indy breezes in the night sky
 I n the winter snowflakes fly
 N ow it's time to put up the Christmas tree
 T he decorations hung up by you and me
 E nd of the day, time to wrap the presents
 R emember to be quiet or Santa won't come.

Gracie-Mae Dudley (9)
Prettygate Junior School, Colchester

Bowgoblins On The Run

Bowgoblins scatter
Wild boars run
Look out archers
Here I come.

Here I am
My name is Link
Face me Bowgoblins
But try not to blink.

The Bowgoblins raise their clubs
High in the air
Here comes Link
Get ready for despair.

Oliver Henderson (8)
Prettygate Junior School, Colchester

A Tiny Cat

Fluffy cat, Fluffy cat, as fluffy as a cloud.
Are you poor as a mouse?
Or rich as a king?
Four little legs
Moving all the time.
Eating fish by the beach.
Crawling slowly, peeking through the houses.
As quick as a cheetah.
A tiny cat, up and down.

Kasope Osikomaiya (7)
Prettygate Junior School, Colchester

The World Of Minecraft

Minecraft, the place I like to be with horses, pigs
and humans like me;
Creepers and zombies kill them too,
Spawn lots of pets to make a zoo.
Make a big house as big as zoo.
Enchant bows and lots of others
to kill the Ender Dragon
and its cores too.

Zach Windsor (9)
Prettygate Junior School, Colchester

Winter

W inter is as cold as an iceberg in the blue sea
 I 'm feeling cold air making my body cold
N ext term it will be summertime
 T he snowflakes trembling down
 E pic children playing in the snow
 R abbits hiding in the trees.

Mallie Watson (7)

Prettygate Junior School, Colchester

Moonlight Flyers

A ngels flying through the night breeze

N ow you see them, now you don't

G et a glimpse and you will see

E very angel is like you and me

L ovely wings, beautiful smile

S ome angels look down at us, some follow.

Serenity Scarlet Walker (10)
Prettygate Junior School, Colchester

Crazy Cautious Coltan!

Surviving!
Everyday lives
Phones and communication
Helps with hospital equipment
Entertains people all day long
Causes death to animals - gorillas
People addicted to technology
People illegally mining
Child workers
Diseases.

Bentleigh Kenyon (10)
Prettygate Junior School, Colchester

Coltan Good Or Bad?

Entertainment
Evolves knowledge
Powers hospital equipment
Tracking people with communication.
Wealth, travel, death, bush-meat, entertainment
People addicted to technology,
Illegal coltan mines
Child warriors
Death.

Aleksander Barakat-Booty (10)
Prettygate Junior School, Colchester

Tortoise

Tortoises are slow, wow as they go,
Why are they so slow?
Tiny little animals eating all the time,
Their shell is so spotty,
Shiny all the time,
Gleaming, glittering, shiny and sparkling.
They're so slow, who knows where they go?

Freya Collison (7)
Prettygate Junior School, Colchester

Winter

W inter is beautiful

I n the cold you can feel it is freezing

N ature is running away

T rembling snowflakes falling from the sky

E pic children skating on the ice

R abbits scrambling in the forests.

Hope Stannard-Rice (7)

Prettygate Junior School, Colchester

Racing Through The Wind

Starting at the start line,
Three... two... one... go!
Off I go riding through the wind,
Halfway now,
People cheering really loud.
But I can't hear a sound
I am aiming for first place
I have won the race!

George Loughton (9)
Prettygate Junior School, Colchester

Dreams

D reams are so magical
R ainbows are so colourful
E xcited in a dream is happiness
A mazing dreams can come true
M agical angels coming into your dreams
S and covering my feet.

Ava Herlihy-Larke (7)
Prettygate Junior School, Colchester

Curious Coltan!

Gadgets
Helps people
Communication and entertainment
Surviving in the wild
Coltan, Coltan, Coltan, Coltan, Coltan
People addicted to technology
Diseases and war
Habitats destroyed
Death.

Abdur-Raheem Iftikhar (10)
Prettygate Junior School, Colchester

Coltan Good... Bad!

Coltan
Powers technology
Good for medical,
Equipment and space shuttles
Saves life and destroys it
Not good for wildlife
Destroys the Congo population
Causes catastrophe
Argh!

Ed Foster (10)
Prettygate Junior School, Colchester

Monkey

Two tiny legs.
Two fast fluffy legs.
His favourite food is banana.
Favourite hobby is eating a banana.
Small monkey teeth.
Skin as brown as a tree trunk.
Monkeys love trees.
Their laugh is silly.

Ali Sat (7)
Prettygate Junior School, Colchester

Coltan Crimes In Congo

Devices
Communicate, us
Thousands upon thousands
Technology brings us good information
Ebola strikes here now today
People addicted to gadgets
Killing the gorillas
Diseases spread
Death.

Sophie Louise Riddiough (10)

Prettygate Junior School, Colchester

Coltan Crimes In Congo

Electronics
Hospital equipment
Communicate with friends
Surviving in the wild
Saves lives but kills people
Diseases spread in mines
Destroying gorillas environment
Illegal mines
Death!

Owen Bardell (10)
Prettygate Junior School, Colchester

Crazy Congo

Coltan
Saves lives
Texting family, friends
Let us travel places
Coltan Technology devices are cool
People addicted to devices
Destroys animals, habitats
People die
Coltan.

Lewis Daniel London (10)

Prettygate Junior School, Colchester

My Snowman

Snow is falling on the ground,
Snow does not make a sound,
Making snowmen round and tall,
Snowman, won't you move at all?
When the sun comes up and down,
My snowman melts into the ground.

Ciarán JS Hinds (9)
Prettygate Junior School, Colchester

Coltan Crimes! Mystery Strikes

Amazing!
Life-saving!
Help us research!
Coltan devices are outstanding!
Coltan, Coltan, help me! Coltan!
Animals are dying now!
Illegal mining now!
Destroys lives!
Death!

Grace Wilkinson (10)
Prettygate Junior School, Colchester

Coltan Crimes Come To Congo

Technology
Evolves knowledge
Surviving in wild
Outstanding products by Coltan
Saves lives and destroys them
Diseases are spread crazily
Animals are dying
Illegal mines
Death!

Phoebe Jones (10)
Prettygate Junior School, Colchester

Coltan Strikes Congo

Technology
Saves lives
Truth and justice
Coltan's help is massive
Helps people find their fortune
Ebola strikes him now
Coltan strikes mayhem
Life ending
Precarious!

Sanjit Veeramreddy (10)
Prettygate Junior School, Colchester

Panther

Teeth as sharp as blades
Lots of fierce claws
One long dark tail.
Pouncer, climber, hunter.
Black as the night.
Wild and pouncing to eat.
As pitch-black as a house with no lights.

Reuben Jack Taylor (7)
Prettygate Junior School, Colchester

Coltan Killer

Tech
Saves us
Virtual reality environments
Coltan makes phones, really!
It kills and it heals
Coltan kills small children
Destroying the environment
Kills us
Conflict.

Jacob Reed (10)
Prettygate Junior School, Colchester

Coltan Crimes

Technology
Is amazing
Coltan saves lives
Science equipment and rockets
Wealth for technology companies
Diseases to all animals
Child abuse labour
Destroys lives
Death!

Charlotte Holmes (11)
Prettygate Junior School, Colchester

Young**Writers**

Coltan

Surviving
Hospital equipment
Good for entertainment
Help us power phones
Coltan good, Coltan is bad
Not good for wildlife
Death and war
People addicted
Diseases.

Grace Alden (10)
Prettygate Junior School, Colchester

78

Coltan Crimes

Coltan
Helps us,
To save lives,
and to work planes
People are addicted to phones
Coltan destroying forest homes
And children's lives
Diseases too
Death.

Emily Windsor (10)
Prettygate Junior School, Colchester

Coltan

Coltan
Makes contact
Saving lives every day
Making people say hey
Coltan is good but bad
Millions dead in Congo
Destroying gorilla's homes
Making war
Death!

Abi Barratt (10)
Prettygate Junior School, Colchester

Coltan Good And Bad

Kills
Young children
Mining for Coltan
For our mobile phones
Which is destroying the wild
Helps us in England
Evolving our knowledge
Helps us
Survive.

Amelia Chatten (10)
Prettygate Junior School, Colchester

Coltan Crimes

Technology
Saves lives
Makes new friends
Play PS4 with buds
Powers all of our phones
Children addicted to gadgets
And diseases spread
Death!

Owen Ross (10)
Prettygate Junior School, Colchester

Unicorn

It has lots of fluffy fur.
It has a pretty horn.
A unicorn is like candyfloss.
A unicorn is like a fluffy cloud.
A unicorn is as pretty as a young child.

Phoebe Ella Coles (7)
Prettygate Junior School, Colchester

Under The Autumn Tree

A pples falling

U mbrellas rising

T oppling trees

U nder the autumn tree

M angoes harvested

N ettles growing.

Thomas William Harvey (9)

Prettygate Junior School, Colchester

The Rabbit

Four bouncy legs,
Two floppy ears,
one wiggly tail
Jumping, running, twitching
Cute and lovable,
Like a miniature kangaroo.

Lilly-Mai Webster (7)
Prettygate Junior School, Colchester

A Parrot

One noisy beak
Two flappy wings
One squawky voice
Hanging, gripping, shrieking
Soft and fluffy
Like a colourful rainbow.

Riley Michael Abrehart (7)
Prettygate Junior School, Colchester

My Life Is Amazing!

Hello, my life is amazing,
Servants I have them.
So I spend my life lazing,
I have a large ruby-red gem,
That shines in the light.

Toys coming out of my ears,
I have a big bed to sleep in at night,
So I never cry tears.
I am famous,
And I am proud.
I live in Vegas,
Which is like living on a cloud.

I'm a diver
And live near a building site,
So I'm very handy with a screwdriver,
I'm also a weightlifter, I heave with all my might.

If you thought all of this was true,
Then you must be new,
As I'm just an ordinary girl,
Who loves to twirl...

Georgia Sydney Elizabeth Richards (11)
Riverside Primary School, Hullbridge

Super Seasons

I am a season,
I love animals and flowers.
The sun and rain come together.
Colours everywhere,
Green shoots are sprouting
I am as colourful as a rainbow.
What season am I?

I am a season,
I love colourful leaves,
I am full of wind, and fallen leaves.
I am the season before winter.
I am full of leafless trees as bare as a cloudless night.
What season am I?

I am a season.
I love sand and sea.
The sun is always shining
I come after spring.
I am the season for barbecues.
My days are normally hot.

I am full of sunshine, as bright as a new light bulb.
What season am I?

I am a season,
I love snow and ice.
Snow is falling,
Fires are lit,
People inside.
I am as cold as ice,
What season am I?

Ruby May Bence (9)
Riverside Primary School, Hullbridge

Football Madness

F un, fun, fun, what you should have

O n or off the pitch you're still part of the team

O nce I was a little boy and playing football was my dream.

T ackling, teamwork and target shots are key to the game.

B est to make sure the team's kits are different and not the same

A ll the parents support us and cheer really loudly when we score.

L isten and learn is what we do best to make our team talks work!

L ast but not least the most important thing is to have fun!

Ronnie Durussel (9)

Riverside Primary School, Hullbridge

Love, Family And Friendships

R elationships are precious as can be!

H aving a wonderful time with friends around

Y ou always need a friend to talk to

M aking good jokes and sharing your love

E njoy the life you have, don't waste it.

C aring is sharing, so make the world a better place

R elaxing with friends is a joy!

A s years go past a friendship could last

F amily and friends are what you need when times are rough

T omorrow is a new day for friendships to grow.

Jessica Doyle (10)
Riverside Primary School, Hullbridge

A Guide To Minecraft

M is for mining to search for treasure

I is for inventory to check things are safe

N is for nicking other people's loot

E is for eggs that hatch and attack

C is for crafting whatever you like

R is for revealing the things you have found

A is for adventures in a different land.

F is for finding caves that are hidden

T is for TNT when you blow up your house.

Roman Foster (8)

Riverside Primary School, Hullbridge

Autumn Day

The leaves blow in my face
like a small hurricane of wind.
The crisp, but not frosty
air enlightens my sense of humour,
Changes my inspiration along
with my imagination in my head.
A pony is running through the
wet, silky, long grass.
A long-necked giraffe comes over
to the nice long healthy tree,
And is biting a crisp leaf.
On a special autumn day.

Emma Potter (10)
Riverside Primary School, Hullbridge

Rhymecraft

Minecraft is like Rhymecraft
But really they are both daft.

Building block houses and
Do this with my mouse,
Animals on a farm,
Not as scary as Steve the spider or ghost riders.

Forest and trees are cut down to build.
It ends up looking like an empty field.
The Rhymecraft world is full of fun,
The bricks and house weigh a tonne.

Hollie Durussel (7)
Riverside Primary School, Hullbridge

Mining Like A Maniac

Mining at midnight.
Mining in the morning.
Snoring in the noon.
Mining like a maniac.
Mining, mining, rhyming while I'm mining,
Mining like a maniac.
Oh look, a figure in the dark.
Four legs,
No arms.
Oh no! Is it what I think?
Kaboom! I'm dead, I'm done.
The pain was like I had been shot with a gun.

Alfie McDonnell (10)
Riverside Primary School, Hullbridge

Builder Bricks

Minecraft,
Rhymecraft,
What we like to build and craft,
The diamond bricks shine in the sun,
The wrong type of bricks make your mouth go numb.
You can build a house, with a little mouse.
Enderman rules the world tonight,
making everyone sleep in fright.
Minecraft,
Rhymecraft
What we like to do is craft.

Hannah Grace Mealing (8)

Riverside Primary School, Hullbridge

All About Dance

How to dance, your first step forward, side,
together
The timing, one... two... three...
Try and guess what it is?
Here's a clue
One of the ballroom dances
And it begins with a 'W'

Two week dancers learn a new step.
Step,
The whisk,
Turn, leg back, chase.
Dance the waltz with me!

Tyne Every (9)
Riverside Primary School, Hullbridge

Lego Bricks

I like to play with bricks and make big sticks,
I have fun making a gun with multicoloured Lego
bricks!
I like to make fast cars
and drive them around the room.
I like to make tall rockets
and fly them to the moon!
When it is time to pack away
and my rockets return from space,
I like everything tidy in its place.

Morgan Hunt (9)

Riverside Primary School, Hullbridge

Friendship

Roses are red,
Violets are blue,
Our friendship is special, just me and you.
We smile, we laugh, we sing, we play, we cry,
We dance and that is what our friendship is today.

Roses are red,
Violets are blue,
Our friendship is special.
Just like me and you.

Kaysie Colston (11)
Riverside Primary School, Hullbridge

Minecraft

M icky loves to build
 I t's his favourite thing
N ext to eating pizza
E ither that or
C hocolate
R ight now he'd rather be
A t home working on his world
F irst making a castle
T hen colouring it blue.

Micky Woods (11)

Riverside Primary School, Hullbridge

Homework

H omework
O h no, not again!
M aths is my tricky one
 E nglish is not much better
W hy does it keep on coming?
O nly one piece to go
R eading I just about can handle
K eep going, I'm almost finished.

Zach Land (10)
Riverside Primary School, Hullbridge

Building And Digging

M ining down block by block

I shall

N ever stop

E ach of us

C raft a pick

R ich we shall become

A fter that let's have some

F un and celebrate

T ill the sun goes down.

Ralph Hall (7)

Riverside Primary School, Hullbridge

Friendship

Friendship is close to your heart,
Like your family.
You can never give up on them.
They can never give up on you.
So when you see your friends care for them,
Cherish them and respect them.

Kayla Harris (9)
Riverside Primary School, Hullbridge

My Dog Bella

My dog Bella is furry and funny,
She keeps me warm like a bunny,
Even though she is quite fluffy,
She is my golden jewel,
I love her so much I gave her my favourite ball.

Lilia Gilbert (10)
Riverside Primary School, Hullbridge

Look Down And Up

M ysterious

 E merald-green tails

 R eds and blues

M agical

 A tlantis

  I llusion

 D eep underwater

 S inging.

Daisy Land (7)

Riverside Primary School, Hullbridge

The Joke That Went Wrong!

There once was a boy who was as naughty as a
cheeky monkey
And a girl who was as sensible as a teacher.
They were brother and sister.
Tommy was their hamster.

Now they knew they were naughty, they knew it
was bad
If they gave the hamster chocolate, mum would be
sad!
Mum wasn't looking, they snatched the chocolate
from the cupboard
It was a gold mine of delicious sweet treats!

Creeping and sneaking they climbed the stairs
To where Tommy waited unaware,
Carefully they crumbled the crunchy chocolate
It fell like drops of gold.

Nibble, nibble, crunch, crunch
Tommy the hamster began to munch.

'Oh no, look at Tommy, look at his tummy
Something going on here is very funny.'
Tommy was getting fatter, he was getting bigger.

Bigger and bigger and bigger and bigger
Boom, pop, bang and *pow!*
'Oh my goodness, what's happening now?'

Poor old Tommy was now in pieces.
Let's hope he rests in peace.
'What was that?' shouted the mother below
'Nothing Mum, you don't need to know!'
Then Mum stormed in, as angry as a lion.
She knew those cheeky children were lying.
So, they told the truth and got three months 'time'
In-house prison,
And never had chocolate again.

Jack Oscar Harding (9), Samuel Reece Woodcock, Lucia Russell, Taylor & Alfie Pyner
Willowbrook Primary School, Hutton

The Cafe Disaster

There once lived a boy as naughty as can be,
Who once put a bee in his mum's tea.
They moved house one day,
They were there to stay,
Well that was what his mum had thought.
They opened a cafe downstairs in the house,
Which he once tried to sabotage with a mouse.
The he-devil was planning a trick so bad,
That they would all go mad.
He was going to set the bread on fire,
No one would know his true desire.
So he went and set his evil plan,
And went to a person called Dan.
To get all of the materials he shall need,
From Dan (who was drinking some mead).
He started to set up his plan,
He worked as quick as a sprinting man.
He set the bread on fire,
Red flames shot higher and higher.
But it would not stop spreading,
Then they heard a *bing*.

All they could do was quickly run,
The bing only meant the oven was done.
But then all the firemen appeared,
Just as Ben had feared.
Now it would be safe,
And they were all fine.
'Kevin,' she screamed at the top of her lung,
He ate all the bread even though it was covered in dung.
As mad as a hatter Ben's mum shouted out,
'You wasted a thousand pounds worth of trout!'
So they had to move back to Brentwood,
And start saving up to go to Hollywood.
But he will never stop being bad,
Or stop driving his poor mother mad.

Alexia Kendall (10)
Willowbrook Primary School, Hutton

The Locker Of Farts

Once in a massive school there was a young boy called Billy.
He was really smart and he wasn't silly.
Every day Billy got bullied by a boy called Big Brad.
He was very rude and very bad.
Billy got chucked in the locker of farts!
And a few seconds later he began to barf.
Billy knew he had to get revenge.
But how?
A while later he thought of a plan, it was very funny.
It was very bad.
All to get revenge on Big Bad Brad.
Billy came to school really early.
To spray a nice-smelling air freshener.
It was a spring flower flowing through the air.
When little Billy was about to get bullied by Big Brad.
Brad smelled the air freshener.
He started to get mad.
Wham! Big Brad slammed the door angrily.
'Did you do this Billy? Because if you did you're acting really silly!'

Billy said, 'No,' with a grin on his face.
So then he got punched like getting hit with a
mace.
After school Billy came home with a black eye.
It was really sore. It was as black as a fly.
'What happened Billy?' asked his mum.
She listened closely and comforted her son.
Mum was super and saved the day
She went to the school to have her say
And happily ever after Big Brad got expelled.

Aryan Hussain (9)
Willowbrook Primary School, Hutton

My Teacher Ate My Homework

Hello, my name is Tom Aston.
You might think I'm a huge jerk
Because I don't like doing my homework.
I never seem to get it back.
But one day my teacher came in with a big sack
And she remarked.
'This is your homework for the week
You just might want to take a peek.'
There were lots and lots of homework just for me!
'Oh no, how could this be?'
There was so much work in my homework book.
It was squished like a full sandwich I couldn't look
So I spent the day in bed
I didn't stop doing my homework until I was nearly dead.
Then... done!
Wahooooo!
I handed it in the next day.

Then we went out to play
But I stayed in,
Watching my teacher, like an owl
She was a careful detective marking my homework.
But then...
Chomp!
She ate my homework!
I rushed into the room and shouted, 'Ha, I caught you!'
Yes, I finally caught her eating my homework.
I had proof.
Now I know why she is as fat as a pig!

Kai Jassy-Catton (9)
Willowbrook Primary School, Hutton

The Boggy Doggy

Once there was a little boy who had a pet dog.
He and his mum took him on a walk,
Splash, he jumped in a bog.
Mum roared, 'You silly dog!'
They walked home with the boggy dog through
loads of fog.
The dog was as brown as a monkey.
And as green as grass.

He was as wet as water.
The dog barked as loud as thunder.
He was renamed Boggy because all he did was get
himself soggy!
Nervously they took him on a walk once again
Guess what he did...
He jumped in a bog.
Which means he is now a soggy, boggy doggy.

The dog zoomed off as fast as an aeroplane.
Detectives they were, searching for hours.
They followed footprints, but that led to a random
dog.

They asked people if they have seen a chocolate Labrador.
Everyone said, 'No!'

Later that month someone told them that they found their dog.
They spent so much money on treats for the dog.
The dog had the best life ever after that.

George Holloway (9)
Willowbrook Primary School, Hutton

Don't Eat The Sweets

Once there was a little girl called Daisy
She was naughty and super lazy.
She wasn't allowed toffee
It would make her tooth ache like a knife plunging in her mouth.
But one day she did...
She snuck some toffee when she said she would help her mum unpack the shopping.
Suddenly, her mouth was stuck shut
Her mum said, 'Are you done?'
She shook her head.
Her mum saw that she'd eaten the toffee,
Daisy was as scared as a mouse!

'You should have listened to me!' said her bossy mum
She tried saying sorry with her mouth closed but she couldn't.
She went to the dentist again and the dentist said
'No more sweets, no fizzy drinks!'
'Mum, you are so unfairrrrrr!'

Crack!
The windows smash
The mum said, 'You are paying for those, they were as expensive as a diamond.'

Amelia Pixie Harding (9)
Willowbrook Primary School, Hutton

The Boy Who Likes Football!

There was once a boy and football was his game.
He played lots of matches and people thought he
was lame.
His friends always got man of the match,
But he was fine with that.

One mystical night when the stars shone bright
Like diamonds in the sky.
The boy awoke to his surprise
Some football boots lay at the foot of his bed.
They were glowing as brightly as a glow stick.

Next day was match day and he wore his new
shoes
Suddenly, he was as fast as fireworks in the sky.
As the leaves went by he assisted a brilliant goal!
Two seconds later he scored the goal of a lifetime.
He was a hero.

Bang! Crash!
A slide tackle knocks him over
And the shoes fly into the air
Never to be seen again.

They disappeared as quick as lightning.
But for once he got man of the match.

Dylan Hutchins (9)
Willowbrook Primary School, Hutton

Another Day In Minecraft

M ine, eat, sleep and build, just another day of work

I n the day you build and play, but in the night you fight

N ew updates every so often, cool new stuff like llamas and mansions

E ndermen, teleporting up and down, so I wouldn't suggest hanging around!

C reepers hissing behind your back, it's almost like they've got freaking backs

R eproducing, done by breeding, have you tried golden apples? They are great for healing.

A fter a while, you'll be OP. But that doesn't mean you can't first punch another tree!

F ind monuments deep in the ocean, just watch out for guardians, they cause a lot of commotion, so I'd recommend bringing a potion.

T NT, totally deadly, if you use it the price will be heavy.

Tim Baygeldi (8)
Willowbrook Primary School, Hutton

The Missing Purse

There once was a boy called Tom,
Who didn't like his dad and mum.
Tom's hair was black like a deep dark tunnel,
With curls that always were in a muddle.
He was always upstairs in his smelly room,
It was like a pit of doom!
He liked to steal his parents' money,
Tom thought it was very funny.
Sneaking, Tom snatched his mum's purse and hid it in under his rotten bed,
When mum woke up, she discovered her purse had disappeared from under her head.

'Aaaarggh!'
'My purse has gone, Tom come downstairs now!'
Pow!
Tom jumped out of bed and flew down the stairs like Superman!
'Where's my purse?' Mum shouted
'I stole your money for sweets and games'
'You're grounded for two whole months,' Tom's mum exclaimed!

Sunni Bhundia (9)
Willowbrook Primary School, Hutton

The Wrath Of The Peas!

There was once a little boy called Bob
He was as thick as a plank.
He loved cars and dogs and lego,
But he *hated* peas!
Peas were balls of poison,
Peas were like bogies from a cow!
But now it was meal time
Chomp, chomp, crunch, crunch
He began to eat up his lunch.
He left the green corner of his plate
He gave it to the dog before it was too late
His mum came in raging like a tornado.
She glanced at his plate she shouted
'Wow Bob, you ate your peas
I am really pleased.'
Splat, splosh, slosh
From behind her back Bob saw the dog's vomit
attack
It was green and oozing
It was monster slime!

Mum was so angry she exploded
Bang, pow, boom
Now there was blood all over the room.
Bob was sad, Bob was crazy mad.
How would he explain this all to his Dad?

Megan Lee (9)
Willowbrook Primary School, Hutton

Alien Teachers

There was a young lad called Fred,
Who was a lying machine and as cheeky as a
monkey.
When at school, daydreaming was all he did
He imagined teachers were aliens from the past
Who owned laser guns that shot him with a blast!

He told the world that's what they were
And called one 'Green Blob' as he was covered in
fur.
That's how they found out that he insulted all the
staff
They told him to wash the roof, the floor and the
bins
And loads of other sorts of things!

He worked late through the night
And then he had a humongous fright.
To see the teachers walking out
To meet their leader General Sprout
He was flying a UFO
He was right about them but no one would know!

Oscar Amos (9)
Willowbrook Primary School, Hutton

The World's Best Prankster

There was a boy who liked to prank his big sister
and one day he did the biggest prank ever!
Ben was a cheeky monkey so he put a mouse in
Katie's room.
Katie likes doing homework so Ben, the evil
creature, made the mouse eat it.
Nibble, nibble, crunch, crunch
Slowly, slowly the mouse grew and grew and grew
What on earth was on that paper, no one knew!
Or did they?
Ben ran screaming from the room
As scared as a baby
Out came his sister from her hiding place
Laughing at Ben, a smile on her face.
What a sly fox.
The growing potion she had hid on the paper did
the trick.
Ben would never prank her again
Handing the title of 'World's Best Prankster' to his
big sister.

Cody Parish (9)
Willowbrook Primary School, Hutton

The Wonderful Cat

The cat sat on the fat hat,
But he did not realise that he had sat on the black bat.
The bat was under the hat.
After the cat went off the hat, the bat was squashed!
After that, a big brown dog came into the cat's bedroom.
The cat is always as light as a feather but,
The dog was as heavy as a computer.
The cat was always a silly billy.
I don't know why?
The cat was silly, light and a scaredy-cat.
Let's get back to the story.
Then the dog sat on the floor to talk but,
The same thing happened again but,
This time it was the dog and he sat on the frog.
The cat was grey and the dog is brown.

Jodie McGill (7)
Willowbrook Primary School, Hutton

Animal Attack

'What is going on Mum,' questioned Honey
'I don't know,' replied Mum sounding confused
'Look it's the animals, we saw in Africa,' shouted
Honey
'Don't go outside, I'm calling the police,' stated
Mum.

And so she called the police but they never came
'Nooo, the giraffe is eating my rose bush,'
screamed Mum
'I wouldn't worry about that if I were you,' joked
Honey
'Mmmooovveee!' screamed Mum
A rhinoceros had come through the window
'La, la, la,la,' sang the rhino
'Stop rhino,' said Honey sounding scared.

Maisie Cocklin (11)
Willowbrook Primary School, Hutton

The Magic Island

There I was sailing across the sea,
To try and get to the island of diamonds.
I was the same old girl I always was,
But then I see something sparkling in the mist. It was... Diamond Island!
My eyes were sparkling and shiny.
I stepped out of the boat.
I saw lots of them, golden ones and glass ones,
There were tiny ones and some were huge.
Some were golden, some were glass.
As I got closer they got faster,
It was a funny day today.
I was finding them quite funny,
One of them was shaped like a bunny,
It was made of gummy.

Hannah Baygeldi (7)
Willowbrook Primary School, Hutton

What Am I?

Jumping down on clouds,
whilst you're on the ground shining with the sun
having lots of fun.
Pretty like the sky, kind of like royalty.
No one thinks we're alive, how rude!
Well, I never believed in humans only my rainbows.
Wanna have some fun?

Rainbows look like me.
Wonder what I am?
Here's another clue,
Some fly but I don't
I have a horn,
I love my fans.
Our horns are shiny like silver.
We love to have some fun playing tag or Barbie
dolls.
Wanna have some fun!
What am I?

Skyla Lynch (10)
Willowbrook Primary School, Hutton

Friendship

F riendship is everything to me

R ain is dark and dull

I n a lovely blue sky

E verything friendship means to me and you

N obody hates friendship, everyone loves friendship

D o love friendship, do love friendship

S o, do you love each other, then you'll be sunny not blue

H ave love in each other and have hate in no one

I n love with friendship is the best

P izza may be lovely, but friendship is even more lovelier.

Who could hate friendship?

Faiqa Latheef (8)
Willowbrook Primary School, Hutton

Theoville On Halloween

A big tooth lay there on a cloud,
What's it from? Is it from a greyhound?
Wait no! Could it just be, no!
It's not a monster, silly me.
I hear my door creak!
I hear something shriek!
I see a shadow come up the stairs.
It's her! It's her! It's my mum.
My dad, and my brother, now it will be my sister.
Hello sister
Wait no...
Monster!

Your end is near!
The zombies are here, you are not...
RIP
Who you gonna call? Ghostbusters!
Ha! Ha! Ha!

Theo Pease (8)
Willowbrook Primary School, Hutton

Dads!

He is kind and gentle,
He helps you with your homework,
He is soft and not forgetful,
He always remembers your school plays,
He's so bright,
And when you cry a river,
He comes and picks you off your feet like a brave knight,
He'll tuck you in bed and kiss you goodnight,
He will give up watching football,
just so that you can watch your favourite TV show,
When you're in the dark he'll give you a light,
He's a dad!
He's my dad!

Scarlett Wilkes (10)
Willowbrook Primary School, Hutton

The Bone Gobblers

Once there lived some dogs, a staff, a pug and a
sausage dog!
They're all good friends and to them the fun never
ends!
Their hobbies were all the same, along with their
neighbour, a Great Dane!
One day posters went round,
'Football Club'. (To be found)
That very day the Great Dane started a football
club...
The Bone Gobblers!
The club got famous quick...
One hundred dogs in fact of all different sizes...
And fifty-one subs.

Jessica Foster (11)
Willowbrook Primary School, Hutton

Friendship And Emotion

My friends and emotion
Best friends can disagree.
Friends can have their ups and downs,
But they are still your friends.
Friends are not just friends, they are best friends.

They are kind, they are friends, but they act like family to you.
They are best friends, sometimes they can get mad,
But no matter what they do they are still your friends no matter what.

They are like family!
They are friends and altogether we are happy!

Lily-Maye Attree (8)
Willowbrook Primary School, Hutton

Clouds Are Amazing!

Are clouds fluffy?
Are clouds soft?
Do they look pink and never shrink?
What's behind them, let's go and see.
Hold on tight and come with me!
Unicorns, narwhales, raindrops too
You will have so much to do!
Let's have a dance party at ten o'clock
I'll be watching tick to tock!
Now it's time to say goodbye
Get your hat and jump up high!
And with no whizzing time to spare.
We all jumped up into the air!

Leila Lynch (9)
Willowbrook Primary School, Hutton

The Way To The Big City!

Once there was a giraffe looking for a holiday
Once there was a giraffe bored at his home.
He asked his parents could he go on holiday?
He asked his parents, 'Please oh please, oh please.'
They finally said, 'Yes.'
They booked him a flight,
Then they got his stuff for a mighty flight,
With a flash of lightning, he was away.
He snored through the night, he arrived, he said to himself,
'Can I go home?'

Daisy Marshall (10)
Willowbrook Primary School, Hutton

Rain

When the clouds rain it means a cloud has done
something
and hurt themselves.
When one starts to cry everyone does,
it carries on to different countries.
I can't believe how they do it
I guess that's just what they do.
And when you're walking remember to bring an
umbrella.
Because you never know if it's going to rain
if you don't and it's raining.
You're
going
to
get
wet!

Izzy Proctor (8)
Willowbrook Primary School, Hutton

The Animals

A cat sat on a fluffy mat.

The cat went and sat on the fluffy, funky mat.

A dog sat on a log.

A spotty giraffe starts to laugh,

While the elephant was in the bath.

The orange and black stripy tiger went to bite.

The elephant pointed his trunk as the tiger did a bunk.

The pig did a jig as he giggled along the trunk.

The fox and the frog hid in the hay.

As all of the crazy animals started to run, jump and play.

Olivia Kamin (7)

Willowbrook Primary School, Hutton

My Hates And Likes!

Everyone has hates and likes,
Even adults too.
But my hates and likes are the same,
I hate people pretending to have a cousin.
It can be annoying.
I even hate people talking about me,
Everyone hates that.
What do you like the most?
I like people doing lots of teamwork
Everyone likes that.
I like the idea of respect, do you?
Do you ever like playing?
Because everyone does what they like...

Rachael Kilvington (10)
Willowbrook Primary School, Hutton

Guinea Pigs

G is for giggly guinea pigs
U is for underneath little tunnels
I is for inside small shelters
N is for naughty and mischievous
E is for everything flipped upside down
A is for 'Argh!' screamed Mum as she stepped on a stray poop.

P is for poop all over the cage
I is for incredibly cute
G is for guinea pigs, cheeky but cute!

Ethan Metcalfe (10)
Willowbrook Primary School, Hutton

Bubbles The Dog

Bubbles, keep out of sight,
Be careful he might give you a fright.
But he would never bite until one scary night...

It was a Saturday night when he released his first
ever bite...
He had bitten the most feared knight!
It was a massive fight, a very scary night.
It was a one-hour fight at midnight.
Bubbles came back with a sword in his hand,
and didn't wake until the very next day.

Ronnie Dowrich (10)
Willowbrook Primary School, Hutton

Lost Hat

The cat wanted the big fat rat,
So she asked the batty, black bat to catch it.
The batty, black bat came back,
with the fat rat and the old ginger
cat gave him a fluffy furry hat to thank him.
The batty black bat forgot,
Where the fluffy, furry hat had gone.
So, he asked the happy playful puppy,
to help find his favourite, fluffy, furry hat.
But they both couldn't find the hat.

Rogue Marie Knight (8)
Willowbrook Primary School, Hutton

Gangsta Granny Is Stupid

Gangsta Granny is a gangsta,
She is very silly and sneaky.
Never does as she is told.
Granny robs some jewellery,
Silly old Granny
She was eighty-eight, she had robbed her eightieth ring.
After she had fifty more
Granny is so stupid.
Really I hate granny,
And another and another jewellery store.
She smells really bad,
She smells like rotten cabbage.
Yes I do Ben.

Mia Reisman (7)
Willowbrook Primary School, Hutton

Don't Stare For Someone May Be There...

In the dark by the lark someone is there...

He will see you, he will watch you, ready to scare, so always be aware.

Creeping through the night keeping out of sight ready for a fight.

Mr Right always ready to fright, try with all your might.

Just make sure he doesn't bite, try to stay all right.

If you listen to the blues and if you're sad, don't feel bad.

Because you're mad!

Summer Sky Wild (10)

Willowbrook Primary School, Hutton

144

Angry Animals

Angry animals are on the prowl,
In the night you can hear the wolves howl,
Lions hunt in their pride,
In the grass the leopards hide,
Panthers hunt in the night,
The parrots squawk which causes fright,
Some of them are big
Some are small
You never want to see the tallest of them all,
Remember angry animals are always there,
In the night you shall see them glare.

Matthew Magarinos (11)
Willowbrook Primary School, Hutton

The Cat Sat On A Branch

The cat sat on the branch.

He called, 'I can't get down.'

A bat came and swooped down from a tree and the branch nearly broke.

The cloud was catching a brown furry cat as the rotten branch broke.

Snap! went the branch as it fell on the grass.

'Oh my!' said the dad as he tidied the grass.

'Miaow!' said the cat as they both went upstairs.

Charlie Barber (7)

Willowbrook Primary School, Hutton

What's Your Favourite...?

This is about animals,
Some live in fields, some in stables.
Some have eight arms for catching its prey
And some sting like a ray.
Some live in the ocean,
Some live in motion.
A few have scales,
And a lot have tails.
Some live on the ground like a rat,
And some fly like a bat.
And my favourite animal is a cat.

Benjamin Latchford (10)
Willowbrook Primary School, Hutton

Clouds

There was a puffy fluffy cloud.
That lived up in the bright blue sky,
Making funny shapes
Over my house,
Covering the sun.
Now it's grey.
Rain falling down.
Darker and darker
Lightning flashing like lights
Thunder crashing
The dark thunder clouds rolling away
And the puffy fluffy cloud again is here!

Georgina Chappell (8)
Willowbrook Primary School, Hutton

Art!

Art doesn't have to be a piece of art.
Everyone can do it, you can buy it.
You can paint it and colour it.
And the tip of it can be as dark as midnight.
You can draw whatever you want.
You can do it lightly, gently, as thick as you want.
And if you keep on trying, you will be an artist one day.
Keep on trying your best.

Katie Harris (10)
Willowbrook Primary School, Hutton

Halloween

H ectic monsters

A nnoying creatures everywhere

L ong ago, everyone died

L ow down in the cellar, there are dogs

O ctober everything is eerie

W e see your death is near

E eek! Zombies are here!

E ctoplasm suffocating you

N o one visits because you are dead!

Jack Brown (8)

Willowbrook Primary School, Hutton

Jeff Loves Sweets

Jeff and his mum lived in a horrible house.
Jeff always got told off because
He nicked wallets and bought sweets
One day he went into
The shop and bumped
Into somebody he knew
Jeff stole his wallet like a tiger
And when he came back from school...
His mum found out and he zoomed upstairs.
'Come down now!'
'OK, I will give it back.'

Jamie Willis (9)
Willowbrook Primary School, Hutton

Unicorns

Unicorns jumping over colourful shiny rainbows.
They have sparkly horns like the beaming sun.
And they have long, wavy hair and it is soft with
rainbows coming out of it.
They leap in the wind as they
glide through the sky with their beautiful
wings and their pure white skin so thin.
We are the Unicorns.

Tahlia Anne Cook (9)
Willowbrook Primary School, Hutton

Candy And Unicorn Crush

My mum bought some candy for me when I was at home.
I saw a unicorn fly past my window.
Then I heard a knock on the door.
I opened the door and I saw a Candy Crush Flamer.
They came in and sprinkled flour and talcum powder everywhere.
The candy cane clacked its hook.
And the penny sweets started to bounce.

Rubyrose Carmen-Jane Barlow (7)
Willowbrook Primary School, Hutton

Vacation

It was a dark and gloomy night
But I remember that the sun was bright
And it was fun,
And I saw a bun.
The sun shone in my eyes,
I saw some animals.
We are manimals and it sounds like camels.
Then I went home and my dad picked up the phone.
It was my nan and then he said, 'Hi.'

Tommy Chitty (8)
Willowbrook Primary School, Hutton

Football Is The Best

Football is a sport that everyone loves
When you're in goal you wear protective gloves,
Football is fun, you would know if you played it,
When you play it you wear a football kit,
The kits are all different colours like red and white stripes,
And the Scottish fans use bagpipes.

Frankie Jobson (11)
Willowbrook Primary School, Hutton

My Pet Unicorn

U nicorns, a fluffy and a very nice pet

N o unicorns are bad!

I love unicorns

C oloured different colours

O nly out on sunny days

R ainbows is what they dance on

N o more time but time to sleep

S ee you in the morning.

Ellie Cross (8)

Willowbrook Primary School, Hutton

Steve's Night Out

M ining in the night

 I hear something near

N othing is even there

E ndermen teleporting

C reepers creeping.

R un away Steve!

A flash is nearby

F inding where it came from

T he mobs are coming.

Theo Tsingano (8)
Willowbrook Primary School, Hutton

Goldfish Eyes

I wonder what it is like to see through my goldfish's
eye.
It might be weird because he's not sly!
his eyes are bigger than the moon.
I wonder how he goes to the latroon!
He is my shining knight,
I just wish he could see the light!
I wonder, I wonder.

William Andrew Johnson (10)
Willowbrook Primary School, Hutton

Dogs

Dogs like to roll, when you give them their toy dolls.
Always digging holes searching for moles.
They play with their bone so, they are not alone.
They eat their meat after licking their feet.
When they like to keep their stuff, they always go to sleep with it.

Teddy Fleming (10)
Willowbrook Primary School, Hutton

Seasons

Seasons, some are dark,
Some are bright.
Some shine through the night,
Some are good enough to fly a kite.
Summer is hot.
Winter is cold.
Autumn leaves crunch under your feet,
Spring, when the flowers bloom.
Summer is coming soon!

Sophie Elizabeth White (11)
Willowbrook Primary School, Hutton

Fantastic Fish

I have a fish,
I wonder if it has a wish,
So in front of it, I put a lucky charm,
Thinking it would do no harm
But little did I know.
The lucky charm cracked,
And the luck was hacked.
That was the fate of my fish.

Risviny Thirunavugarasu (10)
Willowbrook Primary School, Hutton

Dinosaurs

The dinosaurs are big with every different colour.
They are funky, fuzzy and weird, scary, fierce
meat eaters that eat herbivores.
The herbivores run away from the meat eaters.
So they don't get eaten.

Daniel Grundon (7)
Willowbrook Primary School, Hutton

My Cat Lost His Candy Hat

My pet cat saw someone wearing my hat.
My mummy had some money.
My fish swam in a dish.
A mole saw a pole.
I saw a funky monkey
The cat was fat.
Someone said we should take a walk in the wood.

Tom Proctor (7)
Willowbrook Primary School, Hutton

Buzzy, Buzzy Bees!

Buzzing little bees
Flying over the seas
Collecting some honey
That gets me some money
Stinging all the time
Which sounds like a crime
How do they do it?
No one will know it!

Farheen Saleel (10)
Willowbrook Primary School, Hutton

Teddies Are The Best

Teddies are fun.
Teddies are fluffy.
They're good to snuggle in the night.
They're lovely and soft.
We all love our teddies.
The children love their teddies
So much!

Amy Tobin (7)

Willowbrook Primary School, Hutton

Friendship Time

Friendship is nice,
It is really right.
You will want to play,
All day and night.
You will have small, big,
Funny, lovely friends.
So play all day!

Athina Kapralou (7)
Willowbrook Primary School, Hutton

The Season Poem

Lovely flowers like a big long carpet
Dried out grass like thick spikes.
Leaves falling like cold snowflakes.
Snow falling like big balls of ice.

Jack Moore (7)
Willowbrook Primary School, Hutton

Nurses

Black shoes,
Dresses and leggings
Flat shoes and badges of their names.
Nurses work lots of hours
Drive home
Really late.

Markella Ntisiou (7)
Willowbrook Primary School, Hutton

A Wonderful Ball

B all
O ut of the world
O utside the treetops
K ick a ball
S tarting so tall.

Nithilany Thirunavugarasu (7)
Willowbrook Primary School, Hutton

Waterfall

Waterfalls are so tall
Waterfalls make a splash
Waterfalls go fast.
Waterfalls are the colour green and blue.

Isabelle Vosper (7)

Willowbrook Primary School, Hutton

My Football Experience

Football is fun, football is great
Football is love, football is life.
But why do I always feel nervous on match day?

Football exists!
It is all hit and miss,
My tummy feels nervous,
My hands are wet,
My body is shaking,
And I begin to sweat.

Then the ground begins to rumble,
and the crowd is cheering,
as my goal comes careering down the line,
into the back of the net.
Then everyone is screaming, 'Goal!'
Yes! Football is the best!

Osman Nuri Aydin (9)
Woodford Green Primary School, Woodford Green

Space

I like to think about space,
Which is a wonderful place.
I look out of my bedroom window to see stars,
I wish I could drive there in my car.
Mercury orbits the sun in eighty-seven days.
That's not enough time to play!
Venus is the hottest planet and has lots of lava,
Maat Mons is the biggest volcano and is the
father.
Mars has a volcano and sand that is red.
Which is the same colour as the duvet on my bed!
Jupiter is an orange and white gas giant,
So when you go there, wear a mask, don't be
defiant.
The second largest planet is named Saturn,
Has swirling gas and the rings make a pattern.
Uranus is the one that is the most freezing and icy,
So when you go there, eat something spicy.
Neptune is very cold and blue,
So if you go there, you might get the flu.
The sun which is bright,
Is not easy to see in sight.

When I look at the moon,
I know it will go soon.
Earth is a beast,
That is having a feast.
I like to think about space,
Which is a wonderful place.

Ali Hasnan Mahmood (9)
Woodford Green Primary School, Woodford Green

I'm Invisible

One normal day,
Just after lunch,
My mum came in,
And chatted to my sister.

Mum couldn't find me!
I looked in the mirror,
Wait, wait, wait,
There's nothing there!

Invisible, invisible!
I was invisible!
Nobody could see me!
What should I do?

Play video games forever?
Prank everybody?
Take toys from shops?
I closed my eyes...

My eyes came back to life,
But I was in my bed,
Wait!
It was just a dream...

Luke Marshall (9)
Woodford Green Primary School, Woodford Green